CHRISTMA

LIVERPOOL

C000119039

Kipper Williams

AMBERLEY

A number of these cartoons originally appeared in the Guardian, *the* Spectator, *the* Sunday Times, Private Eye, Country Life *or* Recharge, *so thanks to all concerned for allowing them to be used again here. Thanks also to E&T magazine for permission to reuse the cartoons on pages 4 and 14. Cartoons on pages 7, 15, 27 and 45 © Paperlink 2016.*

First published 2016

Amberley Publishing
The Hill, Stroud,
Gloucestershire, GL5 4EP
www.amberley-books.com

Copyright © Kipper Williams, 2016

The right of Kipper Williams to be identified as the Author of this work has been asserted in accordance with the Copyrights, Designs and Patents Act 1988.

ISBN 978 1 4456 6360 9 (print)
ISBN 978 1 4456 6361 6 (ebook)

All rights reserved. No part of this book may be reprinted or reproduced or utilised in any form or by any electronic, mechanical or other means, now known or hereafter invented, including photocopying and recording, or in any information storage or retrieval system, without the permission in writing from the Publishers.

British Library Cataloguing in Publication Data. A catalogue record for this book is available from the British Library.

Typesetting and Origination by Amberley Publishing.
Printed in the UK.

RUN-UP
TO
CHRISTMAS

Kipper
Williams

Kipper Williams

KipperWilliams

Gallery of SURREALISM

Kipper Williams

'Across the field, left at the fountain,
over the moor and right at the mountain.'

'Stuffing ... stuffing ...'

Kipper Williams

'This year I'll be heading somewhere hot.'

'Michelangelo, when I asked you to carve...'